DISNEP
Lilo & Stitch
THE OFFICIAL COOKBOOK

MORE THAN 40 RECIPES TO MAKE FOR YOUR 'OHANA

By Tim Rita

INSIGHT
EDITIONS

SAN RAFAEL · LOS ANGELES · LONDON

Contents

Introduction

- - - - - - - - - - - - - -

Aloha! Thank you for joining me on this culinary journey inspired by the out-of-this-world characters from *Lilo and Stitch*, as well as the rich family heritage of 'ohana that the Hawaiian Islands offer. I will be your guide on this flavor tour as we construct and deconstruct some tasty delicacies that are very easy to make and fun for the whole family. If you've watched *Lilo and Stitch*, you know that 'ohana is the Hawaiian word for "family," and your 'ohana can include anyone—your immediate or extended family, your pets, or even the friends you call family.

This cookbook holds a special place in my heart because several of the recipes come from my own 'ohana, inspired by many lū'au and get-togethers with friends. In Hawaiian culture, it is very common for the entire 'ohana to do their part in cooking a meal—from preparing the rice to setting the tables, everyone is involved! I was born and raised on the island of O'ahu, which is just a short skip from the island of Kaua'i, where the *Lilo and Stitch* story takes place. Creating the recipes for this book brought me back to the times I spent as a child going to a lū'au, running around my town, and enjoying the beach. But the food . . . oh the food! The food is what brings me back to my childhood every time—walking into my mama's kitchen, just smelling the aromas from all of the different dishes she made. One day it would be Filipino, next it would be traditional Hawaiian, then she might finish the week off with an amazing Indonesian pot roast.

Hawai'i is known for being a melting pot of flavors. It started all the way back in the mid-nineteenth century when the sugar industry began in Hawai'i. With that came opportunities for many immigrant workers from around the world—thousands of people from China, Portugal, Japan, the Philippines, Korea, and Puerto Rico made Hawai'i their home to provide for their families and start new lives. To this day, those very cultures and people influence how we eat on the Hawaiian Islands. Most of my dishes, including the ones in this cookbook, are based on the family recipes passed down to me, blended with new additions and fun flavors from my favorite Disney movie—in the same way all the different characters in *Lilo and Stitch* come together to bring a little bit of their backgrounds to the community.

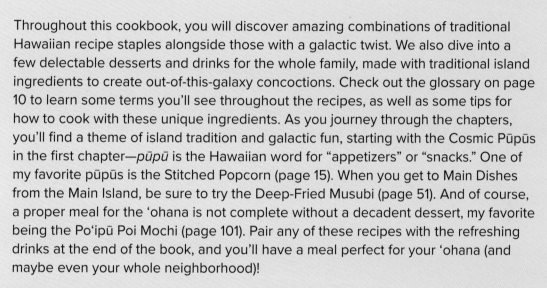

Throughout this cookbook, you will discover amazing combinations of traditional Hawaiian recipe staples alongside those with a galactic twist. We also dive into a few delectable desserts and drinks for the whole family, made with traditional island ingredients to create out-of-this-galaxy concoctions. Check out the glossary on page 10 to learn some terms you'll see throughout the recipes, as well as some tips for how to cook with these unique ingredients. As you journey through the chapters, you'll find a theme of island tradition and galactic fun, starting with the Cosmic Pūpūs in the first chapter—*pūpū* is the Hawaiian word for "appetizers" or "snacks." One of my favorite pūpūs is the Stitched Popcorn (page 15). When you get to Main Dishes from the Main Island, be sure to try the Deep-Fried Musubi (page 51). And of course, a proper meal for the 'ohana is not complete without a decadent dessert, my favorite being the Po'ipū Poi Mochi (page 101). Pair any of these recipes with the refreshing drinks at the end of the book, and you'll have a meal perfect for your 'ohana (and maybe even your whole neighborhood)!

My favorite part about cooking and creating new dishes is sharing them with my family and friends. In this cookbook, I'll show you how to recreate these incredible dishes in the comfort of your own kitchen. And while some of the ingredients and techniques may seem unique to you, I promise these recipes are accessible for even the newest of chefs. Let's begin this delicious tour of Hawai'i through the prism of *Lilo and Stitch*. Mahalo for joining us, and enjoy the ride!

Glossary

'Ahi - tuna fish

Hawai'i - a group of islands in the Pacific Ocean

Hoaloha - friend

'Inamona - relish made of the cooked kernel of kukui (candlenut)

Kālua - to bake in a ground oven

Kaua'i - island in Hawai'i

Keiki - children

Kōkua - to help

Kumu - teacher

Laulau - leaf-wrapped bundle of food

Lawai'a - fisherperson

Lomilomi - to knead or rub

Lū'au - contemporary name for a Hawaiian feast;
also the term for kalo or taro leaves

O'ahu - island in Hawai'i

'Ohana - family

'Ono - delicious

Pā'ina - a party or a celebration

Po'ipū - beach in Kaua'i; also the term for
"crashing waves"

Poke - to slice or cut; also name of local dish

Pūlehu - to broil

Pūpū - appetizer

Cooking Tips and Tricks

- To prepare the lūʻau (or kalo or taro) leaves: Wash the lūʻau leaves thoroughly, one by one, the same way you would clean any vegetable before cooking. Then, chop off the bottom stem that extends past the bottom of the leaf. Chop the stem into ½-inch pieces and set aside.

- To prepare the ti leaves: Wash the ti leaves and pat dry. Remove the thickest vein that runs through the center of the ti leaf. (Note: Removing this vein allows the ti leaves to be more pliable and easy to fold so you can use it to wrap the fillings.) Set aside.

- Steak cooking temperatures: for rare, 120°F; medium rare, 130°F; medium, 135°F; medium well, 140°F; and well done, 150°F.

- Some of the ingredients you may see are local to Hawaiʻi, but you can find most of the products in the ingredients lists throughout the book at your local Asian grocery store.

- If ʻahi tuna is unavailable in your town, ask your seafood department professional or a sushi chef for their choice of fish that they have available for the raw dishes.

- If the recipes require specific ingredients, such as Sugarloaf pineapples, you can most certainly use the traditional ingredients, such as pineapples, that your grocery store carries.

- As a general rule of thumb, it's safer to add too little of an ingredient than too much. You can always add more but you can't take out. For example, if you add too much spice to a dish, you can't really reverse what you did. But if you add a little at a time, you can easily add more spice if necessary.

CHAPTER
1
COSMIC PŪPŪS

Stitched Popcorn

Lilo's life may have been turned upside down, but she still knows how important it is to remember her family and her Hawaiian culture. As she reminds Nani, 'ohana means "family." And what better way to spend time with your family or friends than with a movie and big bowl of popcorn? Inspired by the actual Hawaiian tradition of adding extra seasoning (such as soy sauce and furikake seasoning) to movie-theater popcorn, called Hurricane Mix, this is one snack you won't want to miss!

Prep and Cook Time:
10 minutes

Servings: 4 to 5

One 4-ounce bag microwave popcorn popped, or 1½ cups traditionally prepared popcorn

2 tablespoons salted butter, melted

½ teaspoon soy sauce

2 tablespoons furikake seasoning (a mix of white sesame seeds, black sesame seeds, toasted seaweed, sugar, and salt)

1 to 2 cups Japanese rice crackers (e.g., arare or mochi crunch)

1 small bag red-hot cheese puffs

1. Put all of the popped popcorn in a large, resealable plastic bag.

2. Place the melted butter and soy sauce in a mixing glass and stir gently. Then add that mixture over the popcorn in the bag.

3. Add the furikake seasoning and rice crackers to the popcorn.

4. Seal the popcorn bag completely and shake it up until all of the ingredients are mixed together as evenly as possible. Then pour the popcorn mixture from the bag into a large bowl.

5. Take the red-hot cheese puffs and place the contents in a separate plastic bag. Seal the bag and gently crush the cheese puffs thoroughly.

6. To serve, sprinkle the cheese puff dust evenly over the popcorn in the bowl.

The One Time Lilo and Stitch Made Poke

Stitch can make a mess of anything. Even when he's trying to be careful, things still seem to end up broken. Luckily, this poke is one dish where making a mess is encouraged! In Hawaiian, *poke* actually means "to cut," so the more you (or Stitch) break apart the meat and veggies in this recipe, the better!

Prep and Cook Time:
15 minutes, plus 2 hours to refrigerate (if desired)

Servings: 4 to 5

1 pound fresh 'ahi steak, cut into bite-sized cubes

¼ cup soy sauce

2 avocados, cubed

¼ cup chopped green onions

¼ cup chopped Maui onion or sweet onion

2 teaspoons sesame oil

1 teaspoon grated fresh ginger or ground ginger

1 Hawaiian chile pepper (e.g., bird's eye chile), diced

Sea salt

3 pinches sesame seeds

2 teaspoons 'inamona, or 1 micro-planed macadamia nut

1. In a large bowl, combine the 'ahi steak, soy sauce, avocados, green onions, Maui onion, sesame oil, ginger, Hawaiian chile, sea salt to taste, sesame seeds, and 'inamona, and mix together gently.

2. Cover and refrigerate the poke mixture for 2 hours, if desired.

3. The poke can be served many ways: on its own, with hot steamed rice, or with your favorite type of chips.

Pro Tip: Or you can be like me and dig in right after mixing. It's so good, I normally can't wait to eat it!

Galactic Kebabs

The Galactic Federation is made up of creatures from all over the universe. Although they all look different, they work well together—just like the ingredients in these tasty kebabs. The peppers, ginger, and chicken in this recipe may not seem like they'd be a good fit, but it turns out they're stronger together than they are apart!

Prep Time: 15 minutes, plus 1 hour to marinate

Cook Time: 12 to 15 minutes

Servings: 4 (12 skewers)

½ cup sriracha hot sauce

½ cup soy sauce

¼ cup lehua honey (Hawaiian honey made from lehua blossoms)

¼ cup apple cider vinegar

1 tablespoon rice vinegar

¾ cup sesame oil

1 tablespoon minced fresh ginger

4 cloves garlic, minced

2 pinches sea salt

2 pinches freshly ground pepper

1¼ pounds skinless chicken breast, chopped into bite-sized pieces

12 white mushrooms, halved

1 large red bell pepper, cut into 1½-inch pieces

1 large green bell pepper, cut into 1½-inch pieces

12 cherry tomatoes

3 tablespoons paprika, optional

3 tablespoons edible gold glitter, optional

Special Supplies

Skewers, wood or metal

1. Whisk together the sriracha, soy sauce, honey, apple cider vinegar, rice vinegar, sesame oil, ginger, garlic, sea salt, and ground pepper in a large bowl.

2. Add the chicken and mushrooms to the marinade mixture. Toss to coat the chicken and mushrooms.

3. Chill in the refrigerator, covered, for 1 hour.

4. Preheat an outdoor grill to medium-high heat (375° to 450°F). (Note: If you don't have a grill, you could use an indoor electric grill or a large frying pan. If you are using a pan, lightly oil the pan with the cooking oil of choice and cook for the same time, or until the chicken is cooked.)

5. Drain the marinade from the chicken and mushroom mixture over a small saucepan. Bring the marinade to a boil over high heat. Reduce the heat to medium-low and simmer for 10 minutes. Pour half of the marinade into a small bowl to baste the skewers.

6. Thread the chicken, mushrooms, red and green bell peppers, and tomatoes onto the skewers.

7. Ensure your grill or pan is clean and lightly oiled. Grill the skewers and brush them with the basting half of the marinade, turning the skewers over occasionally, about 2 minutes, or until the chicken is fully cooked.

8. Right before you serve, if desired, sprinkle a mixture of paprika and edible gold glitter to give a galactic shine to the dish (see pro tip).

Pro Tip: To create edible galactic dust to sprinkle onto your kebabs:

- Take equal parts of paprika and edible gold glitter/powder.
- Mix the two ingredients into a small bowl or empty saltshaker or duster.
- Apply the dust as desired to the kebabs for a fun way to kick up the spice with a galactic sparkle.

Tempura-Style Apple and Carrot Crunch

Cobra Bubbles may be tough on Lilo and Nani, but he just wants what's best for them. This Japanese-inspired tempura dish, which perfectly reflects Hawai'i's wonderful mixing of cultures, is a bit like him: salty and sweet at the same time! That must be why he likes this mix of carrots, apples, and vinegar so much.

Prep Time: 10 minutes, plus 1 hour to refrigerate

Cook Time: 24 minutes

Servings: 4 to 5

4 carrots, peeled and julienned

3 red apples, peeled and thinly sliced with a mandoline

2 teaspoons freshly ground pepper, plus more as needed

¼ cup apple cider vinegar

¼ cup soy sauce

2 egg yolks

2 cups water

2 cups all-purpose flour

2 quarts vegetable oil

Sea salt

Special Supplies

Candy thermometer

1. Take the carrots, apples, pepper, apple cider vinegar, and soy sauce, and add them into a large bowl, mixing well. Refrigerate the mixture for 1 hour.

2. To start the batter, combine the egg yolks and water in one medium-sized bowl. In a separate medium bowl, place the flour. Set aside.

3. In a large frying pan or Dutch oven, heat the vegetable oil to 360°F. (Note: You can check the temperature by using a candy thermometer.)

4. Take a few pieces of carrot and apple at a time and gently dip both sides into the egg and water mixture. Then, dip both sides into the flour bowl.

5. Working in batches, gently place the slices of apple and carrot into the oil and cook for 3 minutes on each side, until golden.

6. To remove the excess oil when fully cooked, let the slices sit on a strainer.

7. Sprinkle lightly with sea salt and pepper to serve.

Kumu Puloki's Hawaiian-Style Coleslaw

Lilo is sometimes late to dance class, but she'd never be late to a meal served by Kumu Puloki. That's because she knows how fast his Hawaiian coleslaw disappears. Like normal coleslaw but with added flavors from the islands, this dish is 'onolicious! 'Ono is a Hawaiian word for "delicious," so translated with island slang, that makes this dish *very delicious.*

Prep and Cook Time:
15 minutes, plus 30 minutes
to refrigerate

Servings: 6

2½ cups shredded green cabbage

1 cup shredded red cabbage

½ cup grated carrots

1 cup small-cubed fresh pineapple

2 green onions, sliced

½ cup sea asparagus (if unavailable, chop 4 spears of asparagus into small pieces)

½ cup chopped Maui onion or sweet onion

¼ cup minced fresh cilantro

1½ tablespoons grated fresh ginger

1 tablespoon olive oil

3 tablespoons rice wine vinegar

1 tablespoon soy sauce

1 tablespoon lehua honey (Hawaiian honey made from lehua blossoms)

2 teaspoons sesame oil

1½ ounces fresh lime juice

Sea salt

1 teaspoon black sesame seeds

4 ounces chicharrones (pork cracklings), optional

1. Combine the two cabbages, carrots, pineapple, green onions, asparagus, Maui onion, and cilantro in a large bowl. Set aside.

2. In a small glass mixing cup, combine the ginger, olive oil, rice wine vinegar, soy sauce, honey, sesame oil, and lime juice. Stir well and pour over the slaw you just made.

3. Stir everything to combine and season with salt to taste.

4. Cover the coleslaw and refrigerate for at least 30 minutes before eating.

5. To serve, sprinkle with black sesame seeds and place the chicharrones in a circle around the edge of the coleslaw, if desired. Enjoy!

Handpicked 'Ohana Fruit Salad

Lilo and Stitch love riding Lilo's bike around town. And it's a good thing, because the ingredients for this fruit salad come from all over the island. When I was growing up in Hawai'i, my neighborhood was a diverse mix of home farmers. It wasn't uncommon for our block to turn into a personal farmer's market on the weekend! The mix of refreshing fruit in this recipe is as diverse as my old neighborhood, and it's perfect for those hot Hawai'i days!

Prep and Cook Time:
30 minutes
Servings: 6

1 whole fresh pineapple with the crown intact

6 island-grown tangerines (or other tangerines available at your grocery store), peeled and stripped of all fiber

1 cup sliced fresh strawberries

6 island-grown mountain apples, sliced (Note: Mountain apples have a similar fleshiness to fruits like fresh lychee and Granny Smith apples.)

One 20-ounce can lychee, drained (often in syrup or water)

1 whole Korean pear or regular pear, sliced into even small ¼- to ½-inch squares

1¼ cups coconut yogurt

½ cup sweetened shredded coconut, toasted and divided

¼ teaspoon vanilla extract

1. Stand the pineapple upright and vertically cut a third of the fruit from one side, leaving the crown attached. Set the cut piece aside for now.

2. Cut strips of the pineapple from the large leftover section, leaving a ½-inch shell, discarding the core.

3. Then cut those pineapple strips into bite-sized chunks and drain any water from the shell of the pineapple.

4. Place the pineapple shell in a serving basket or bowl; set aside.

5. In a large bowl, combine all of the fruit and yogurt, ¼ cup of shredded coconut and the vanilla. Stir everything together gently.

6. Place all of the ingredients into the pineapple shell and sprinkle with the remaining ¼ cup of shredded coconut.

Kokaua Coconut and Chicken Long Rice

As Lilo's guardian, it's Nani's job to take care of Lilo—especially when she's feeling under the weather. This pūpū is the island's favorite form of comfort food. The perfect remedy for a cold, perfect for when it's cold, and oddly enough, delicious when served cold!

Prep Time: 15 minutes, plus 30 minutes to soak

Cook Time: 35 minutes

Servings: 4

4 ounces long rice (bean thread "cellophane" noodles)

¾ pound bone-in chicken thighs

5 cups chicken broth

2 cloves garlic, peeled and smashed

2 tablespoons coconut oil

6 slices (¼-inch-thick) fresh ginger, slightly smashed

1 teaspoon Hawaiian salt

1 cup shredded coconut

6 green onions, thinly sliced

4 coconut shells, halved and cleaned

1. Take the strands of rice and break them in half.

2. Soak the rice for 25 to 30 minutes in warm water. Then drain.

3. Place the chicken in a large pot with the chicken broth, garlic, coconut oil, ginger, and salt.

4. Bring to a boil over high heat. Once boiling, reduce the heat to low and simmer uncovered until the chicken is cooked thoroughly, about 25 to 30 minutes.

5. Skim off any foam caused by the chicken throughout cooking.

6. Transfer the chicken to a cutting board and let cool.

7. Once the chicken is cool, shred the meat the same way you would shred pulled pork or jerk chicken, then remove the skin and bones.

8. Stir the rice into the broth and simmer, uncovered, until translucent, about 6 minutes.

9. Stir in the shredded coconut and green onions, along with the chicken, and serve in the halved coconut shells.

Nani's Spaghetti Salad

Pleakley and Jumba are determined to blend in at Nani's lū'au—at least until they can get their hands on Stitch. Ordering the Spaghetti Salad is a great way to fit in. This traditional Hawaiian dish is usually served at lū'au and neighborhood parties.

Prep and Cook Time:
30 minutes
Servings: 4

One 16-ounce package spaghetti

3 ounces Japanese cucumbers, julienned

½ carrot, peeled and julienned

1 teaspoon sea salt, divided

½ cup water

3 ounces sliced SPAM®, cubed small

1 teaspoon white vinegar

¼ cup mayonnaise

1 pinch freshly ground pepper

1 pinch paprika

1. Cook the spaghetti noodles, as directed on the package, usually about 10 minutes.

2. Strain and cool the spaghetti noodles under cold running water, then set aside.

3. Add the cucumber, carrot, and ½ teaspoon of salt to a small bowl. Mix the ingredients by hand to ensure the salt coats the vegetables completely.

4. Let this mixture sit for 5 minutes, then add the water and swirl the ingredients together to remove the salt.

5. Strain the water out of the vegetables by hand by squeezing them. (Note: This is a very common Japanese method for straining water out of vegetables.)

6. Add the vegetables, noodles, and SPAM® cubes into a large bowl, mixing everything together well.

7. Add the vinegar, mayonnaise, pepper, and the remaining ½ teaspoon of salt.

8. Mix everything together well, sprinkle the paprika over the mixture, and serve.

Kaua'i Sugarloaf Pineapple Salsa

Lilo loves her home, but life on her island hadn't always been easy. Sometimes she wishes it were a bit sweeter. Luckily, the island's Sugarloaf pineapples are perfectly sweet. So sweet you can even eat the core! Any other pineapple will do for this spicy and sweet dish, but it won't be as special. Add just a touch of Kaua'i's own papaya to make this dish perfect!

Prep and Cook Time:
30 minutes
Servings: 12

2 pounds fresh Kaua'i Sugarloaf pineapple, cubed small (regular ripe pineapple is fine, too)

1 small ripe papaya, cubed small

10 Hawaiian pineapple tomatoes (currant tomatoes from Hawai'i) or beefsteak tomatoes, cored and diced

1 bunch cilantro, finely chopped

1 cup finely chopped Maui or sweet onion

3 to 4 jalapeño peppers, seeded and finely chopped

2 ounces fresh lime juice

Hawaiian salt

Freshly ground pepper

Chile pepper water (see pro tip), or red pepper sauce, optional for spice and heat

One 6-ounce bag kalo (taro) chips

1. In a large bowl, add in the pineapple, papaya, tomatoes, cilantro, onion, and jalapeños. Stir to combine.

2. Add the lime juice and toss the mixture to coat.

3. Season the salsa to taste with salt, pepper, and chile pepper water, if using.

4. For best results, allow the flavors to marinate together at room temperature for at least 10 minutes, or chill until serving time.

5. Serve with the kalo chips and enjoy!

Pro Tip: The following ingredients and steps will help you make your own chile pepper water:

6 Hawaiian chile peppers

10 ounces water

4 ounces white vinegar

1 tablespoon Hawaiian or kosher salt

1. Put all of the ingredients into a medium pot and bring to a boil over high heat.
2. Turn the heat down to low to simmer for 5 minutes.
3. Let the mixture cool, then place it in a resealable container of choice (such as a bottle or a jar).
4. You can leave the peppers in the bottle or remove them. The longer the peppers are in the mixture, the hotter it will be, but it will stabilize over time.
5. Keep your chile pepper water in the fridge for up to 6 months.

CHAPTER
2
MAIN ISLAND
MAIN DISHES

Pudge's Peanut Butter, Jelly, and Banana Sandwich

If there's one thing Lilo knows for sure, it's that Pudge the fish controls the weather. And that means keeping him happy! But the stinky tuna fish in her house certainly won't do the trick. Instead, Lilo insists on bringing him a peanut butter, jelly, and banana sandwich—even if it makes her late for dance class!

Prep Time: 10 minutes
Cook Time: 5 minutes
Servings: 4

2 tablespoons unsalted butter, room temperature

8 slices wheat or white bread

1 cup peanut butter, smooth or crunchy

2 ripe apple bananas, sliced (apple bananas are commonly grown in a lot of local Hawaiian backyards, but regular bananas will suffice)

½ cup Hawaiian guava jelly (available online)

Pinch Hawaiian salt or sea salt

Ground cinnamon, for garnishing

1. Spread the butter on the 8 slices of bread, on one side only, and place them butter side down on a cutting board or clean flat surface.

2. Spread peanut butter on top of 4 slices of the bread, and top with the banana pieces.

3. For the remaining pieces of bread, spread with jelly and place them on top of the bananas, jelly side down.

4. Press the sandwiches gently with a spatula to flatten them slightly (and not get butter on your hands!).

5. Heat a dry cast iron or nonstick pan over medium heat. Place a sandwich in the pan and weigh it down with another pan, or simply hold the sandwich down with the spatula. Grill each sandwich for 5 minutes, turn the sandwich over, reweigh it with the pan, and grill for another 5 minutes until crisp on both sides. Alternatively, use a preheated panini press to grill each sandwich for about 5 minutes.

6. Sprinkle with sea salt and cinnamon. Halve each sandwich and serve.

Laulau "From Nani's Lū'au"

If there's one thing that drives Nani up the walls, it's the fact that Stitch is still learning how to take responsibility for his actions. For Hawaiian people, lū'au leaves, or kalo leaves, represent the essential connection between nature and peoples' duty to nature. A great reminder that we all have a duty to care for the earth, this dish is made with the bounty of the land and sea and is wrapped in steamed kalo leaves.

Prep Time: 25 minutes

Cook Time: 3 to 4 hours

Servings: 4 to 6

12 lū'au leaves (available online)

1 pound ti leaves or banana leaves

1 pound pork butt, cubed into ½-inch pieces

½ pound line-caught salmon, cubed into ½-inch pieces

½ pound purple Okinawan sweet potato or purple yams, peeled and cubed

½ pound carrots, cubed

6 red bell peppers, sliced

3 Maui onions or sweet onions, quartered

Hawaiian salt

Special Supplies

Cooking string

1. First, prep the two types of leaves (see the tips on page 11 for how to wash and prepare your leaves).

2. Clean your workstation, then stack 3 to 5 washed lū'au leaves on the counter. (Note: Arrange the leaves so that the biggest leaf is on the bottom and the smallest leaf is on top.)

3. Place a few cubes of the pork butt and salmon in the center of the leaves.

4. Add 2 to 3 pieces each of cubed purple sweet potato and carrots on top, then add 1 sliced bell pepper and 2 quarters of Maui onion. Top with several of the chopped lū'au leaf stems.

5. Sprinkle salt over everything, about a pinch per laulau.

6. Then, use the lū'au leaves to wrap all the fillings in a tight bundle, similar to wrapping a burrito.

continued on page 36

continued from page 35

7. Next, wrap the ti leaves around the lūʻau leaf bundle, just as you would wrap a tamale. Use cooking string to tie/secure the bundle.

8. Put the wrapped laulau (as many that can fit) in a steaming grid, then place the grid in a large enough pot with water. Make sure the water doesn't touch the steaming grid (it cannot touch the laulau). Cover and steam for 3 to 4 hours, or until tender. (Note: Avoid pressing down on the laulaus once they are in the pot, as this will cause them to tear.)

9. Remove the ti leaves before you serve, otherwise the leaves may cause your throat to itch.

10. Serve with your favorite starch or side(s) such as Traditional Lomilomi Salmon (page 81) and the Kokaua Coconut and Chicken Long Rice (page 24).

Jumba's Zapped Pūlehu Short Ribs

Jumba is used to eating a lot—and often! That made the trip to Earth to apprehend Experiment 626 hard. Luckily, he found plenty of food waiting when he landed, particularly in the form of pigs—or wild *buta*. He discovered locals cooking with them *pūlehu*-style, a Hawaiian word for "cooked over fire," and happily enjoyed his fill.

Prep Time: 15 minutes

Cook Time: 10 minutes

Servings: 4

½ cup sea salt

2 tablespoons minced fresh garlic

1 tablespoon cane sugar

2 teaspoons freshly ground pepper

2 teaspoons minced fresh ginger

½ cup soy sauce

1 tablespoon sesame oil

Four 8-ounce boneless short ribs

1. Heat a grill pan or large frying pan over medium heat.

2. Combine the sea salt, garlic, cane sugar, ground pepper, ginger, soy sauce, and sesame oil in a large bowl.

3. Rub the marinade mixture you just made onto the meat.

4. Grill the short ribs for 3 to 5 minutes on each side, until it reaches your preferred char.

5. Serve with your favorite side of vegetables and/or starch.

Pro Tip: I personally like having a side dish of ponzu sauce with my short ribs. You could even take some of your favorite steak sauce and add a few squeezes of sriracha hot sauce for a spicy dip!

Experimental Sweet and Savory Bao Buns

Dr. Jumba Jookiba is definitely a kooky scientist. In fact, his genetic experiments caused so much chaos that he got banned from his own planet! Perhaps he would have been better off experimenting with recipes, like this tasty spread of dim sum buns. There are two different fillings, one sweet and one spicy—blending an array of delicious island flavors in these fun-to-eat bao buns. It's a fantastic mix without any of the chaos of his other experiments!

Prep and Cook Time:
30 minutes
Servings: 10

10 premade bao buns
(can be found online), divided

Savory bao buns

⅓ cup mayonnaise

⅓ cup Dijon mustard

10 butter lettuce leaves or
lettuce cups

1 cup bean sprouts, divided
evenly for 5 buns

2 carrots, peeled, sliced, and
divided evenly for 5 buns

1 cup pork chicharrones, divided
evenly for 5 buns

5 teaspoons lehua honey
(Hawaiian honey made from
lehua blossoms)

Sweet bao buns

1 cup hazelnut spread

2 strawberries per bun,
thinly sliced

25 blueberries

2½ ounces peanut butter chips,
evenly divided for 5 buns

5 pinches Hawaiian salt, or
kosher salt

Banana leaves or ti leaves,
for serving, optional

To make the savory bao buns:

1. Take 5 bao buns and spread the inside of the buns evenly with about 1 tablespoon of each mayonnaise and Dijon mustard.

2. Place the following ingredients inside the buns in this order: 2 pieces of lettuce, 1 ounce of bean sprouts, an even split of carrots, and a chicharron.

3. Then drip about 1 ounce of honey over each bun.

To make the sweet bao buns:

4. Take the other 5 bao buns and spread evenly with the hazelnut spread.

5. Place the following ingredients inside the buns in this order: 2 sliced strawberries, 5 blueberries, and a few peanut butter chips.

6. Sprinkle the salt evenly over each bun.

7. To serve, line a sushi-style platter with banana or ti leaves, if desired, then place the buns on top.

Dawn Patrol Loco Moco

Every surfer knows that the best time to hit the waves is early in the morning, and David is no exception. An experienced surfer, he knows how to work up a good appetite. And the perfect meal to satisfy the hunger of a radical surf session: "dawn patrol." One of the most popular local Hawaiian dishes known outside of the islands, the loco moco was created in the 1940s in Hilo, Hawai'i, by a group of very hungry boys low on money after spending the day at the beach. A hearty meal, this one might even leave Stitch feeling full!

Prep Time: 10 minutes

Cook Time: 30 minutes

Servings: 4

Hamburger Patties

1½ pounds Hawaiian grass-fed ground beef

1 tablespoon Worcestershire sauce

1½ teaspoons sea salt

1 teaspoon garlic powder

½ teaspoon freshly ground pepper

Gravy

1½ cups beef stock

4 teaspoons soy sauce

1 teaspoon Worcestershire sauce

2 teaspoons ketchup

5 teaspoons cornstarch

2 tablespoons unsalted butter, divided

½ Maui onion or sweet onion

¾ cup sliced mushrooms

Assembly

1 tablespoon butter

2 eggs

4 to 6 cups cooked medium-grain Calrose rice

1 green onion, sliced, for garnishing

3 ounces sliced pineapple

To make the hamburger patties:

1. Mix together the ground beef, Worcestershire sauce, salt, garlic powder, and pepper in a large bowl.

2. Form the mixture into patties by grabbing a handful of meat and rolling it into a ball.

3. Press the meat down to flatten it out. Smooth the edges so there aren't any cracks or jagged edges. The patties should come out to at least 1 inch thick. (Note: Try to keep the patties large, since they will shrink when fried.)

4. Heat a large frying pan over medium heat. Fry each side of the patties for about 3 to 5 minutes, or until well done.

5. Set each finished patty on a plate lined with paper towel to catch any extra grease.

continued on page 44

continued from page 43

To make the gravy:

6. Mix the beef stock, soy sauce, Worcestershire sauce, ketchup, and cornstarch in a small to medium bowl.

7. Whisk the mixture until the cornstarch has come off of the bottom of the bowl.

8. Using the same pan that you cooked the meat in, melt 1 tablespoon of the butter over medium heat and add the onions. Cook the onions for about 1 minute, then add the mushrooms and fry for 1 to 2 minutes, or until browned.

9. Melt the remaining 1 tablespoon of butter and add the gravy mix to the pan.

10. Keep stirring the gravy until it begins to thicken and simmer, about 5 minutes.

To assemble the loco moco:

11. In a medium frying pan over medium heat, melt the butter.

12. One at a time, crack in the eggs and cook sunny side up over medium heat (or you can switch it up to your preference!), then set aside.

13. Scoop a generous serving of cooked white rice on a plate.

14. Add one hamburger patty and then drizzle on the gravy. Top it with the egg and garnish with green onions.

15. Place the pineapple slices along one side of the dish, but not in the gravy. That's up to the hungry surfer!

Kiki's Special Saimin Noodles

It may be Nani's job to take care of Lilo, but sometimes Nani needs someone to take care of *her*. That's where her friend Kiki comes in. Kiki is always ready at her coffee shop with her special saimin whenever someone needs a little pick-me-up. Perfect for a cold Hawaiian winter night (70°F. Ha!), saimin is the Hawaiian version of a traditional ramen noodle soup, but here, we use soba noodles for a thicker, heartier soup.

Prep Time: 10 minutes
Cook Time: 15 minutes
Servings: 3 to 4

16 cups water (4 quarts)

1 tablespoon sea salt

One 8-ounce package dried, cold Japanese soba noodles (soba noodles are thicker than your normal ramen and saimin noodles)

4 cups chicken broth

1 tablespoon grated fresh ginger

2 tablespoons soy sauce

Half 12-ounce can SPAM®, sliced

12 thin slices roast pork

½ head Napa cabbage, shredded

2 bunches bok choy, chopped

4 eggs, scrambled or fried

1 bunch green onions, sliced

4 slices kamaboko (Japanese fish cake)

1 whole Japanese cucumber, sliced

1. In a large pot, combine the water and salt and bring to a boil over medium-high heat.

2. Add the soba noodles and boil for 4 to 6 minutes, or until the noodles are al dente.

3. Remove the noodles from the heat and drain. Rinse the noodles under warm water and set aside.

4. In the same pot you used for the noodles, combine the chicken broth and ginger, bringing to a boil over medium-high heat.

5. Reduce the heat to low. Then add the soy sauce, SPAM®, pork, cabbage, and bok choy. Simmer for 5 minutes, or until all the toppings are fully cooked.

6. To serve, place the cooked soba noodles in a large soup bowl and spoon the broth mixture over the top. Add the eggs, green onions, kamaboko, and cucumber over the noodles and enjoy!

Easy-Kine Kālua Pork

No lūʻau would be complete without a roast pig, and there's nowhere better to go for one than Nani's lūʻau, where guests can enjoy a fire show from David followed by a succulent pork meal. Unfortunately, we can't all roast a pig in our backyards, but this dish is an easy-*kine* way to make amazing kālua pork in your own kitchen!

Prep Time: 20 minutes
Cook Time: 12 hours
Servings: 12

4 tablespoons vegetable oil

4 pounds pork shoulder or pork butt

5 to 6 drops mesquite liquid smoke flavor

1 pinch Hawaiian salt

1 head cabbage, optional
(see pro tip)

1. Heat the oil in a large pot over medium-high heat. Dab the pork dry with paper towels, then sear in pot for about 3 minutes per side.

2. Transfer the pork to a 6- or 7-quart slow cooker.

3. Pour the liquid smoke over both sides of the meat and season with the salt.

4. Cover and cook on low heat for 12 hours. (Note: The longer you keep it in the cooker, the softer the meat gets.)

5. Remove the pork from the slow cooker and let rest a few minutes. Then shred the meat, removing bone and fat.

6. Toss the shredded pork and cabbage, if desired (see pro tip), with some of the juices from the slow cooker and serve warm.

Pro Tip: Another popular serving option for this dish in Hawaiʻi is to add a half to a whole head of shredded cabbage in the last 30 minutes of cooking in the slow cooker. Delicious!

Laser-Grilled Octopus Salad

Pleakley's attempt to kidnap Experiment 626 while he was surfing didn't exactly go according to plan. He ended up stranded on a distant beach with an octopus stuck to his head! And Pleakley will be the first to tell you . . . he *hates* octopuses. They're even worse than sharks! But that won't stop him from enjoying this tasty grilled dish. Made with a fusion of Spanish- and Asian-influenced flavors, this dish is truly out of this world.

Prep Time: 30 minutes, plus 30 minutes to marinate

Cook Time: 20 minutes

Servings: 4 to 5

Octopus

10 octopus tentacles

1 cup misoyaki marinade (about 10 percent of the octopuses' weight)

1 tablespoon olive oil

Tomato Salad (Japanese style)

3 celery stalks, sliced

½ cup finely chopped yellow onion

1 teaspoon grated fresh ginger

1 tablespoon soy sauce

1 tablespoon rice vinegar

1 tablespoon sesame oil

1 teaspoon sugar

½ teaspoon Hawaiian salt

1 pinch togarashi (Japanese spice blend)

1 pound beefsteak tomatoes, diced

1 pinch Cajun seasoning mix

1 lemon

2 to 3 cilantro sprigs

To make the octopus:

1. Place the octopus in a freezer bag with the misoyaki marinade. Seal the bag so that it is airtight and leave to marinate in the fridge for about 30 minutes.

2. Heat the olive oil in a griddle on a grill or a stove over medium heat.

3. Remove the octopus from the marinade and cook on the griddle until charred on all sides, about 3 to 5 minutes per side.

To make the tomato salad:

4. While the octopus is cooking, whisk together the celery, onion, ginger, soy sauce, rice vinegar, sesame oil, sugar, salt, and togarashi in a small bowl until the dressing is combined.

5. Arrange the tomatoes evenly on a plate and spoon the dressing over the tomatoes.

6. Plate the grilled misoyaki octopus in the center on the tomatoes, top with the Cajun seasoning, and garnish with a squeeze of lemon and the cilantro. Enjoy!

Deep-Fried Musubi

Times may have been hard for Lilo and Nani, but that didn't mean they couldn't eat well. This tasty SPAM® dish is perfect for the duo on the go. Just leave it marinating and cook it up when you get home from a shift! For those who never thought a SPAM® musubi could be fancy, behold the Deep-Fried Musubi!

Prep Time: 15 minutes, plus 1 hour for chilling

Cook Time: 20 minutes

Servings: 8 to 10

Musubi

12 ounces SPAM®

¼ cup oyster sauce

¼ cup soy sauce

½ cup brown sugar

8 to 10 eggs

Nori roasted seaweed, cut into halves or thirds

6 cups cooked Calrose rice

8 to 12 thin slices pickle

Paprika for garnishing, optional

Batter

2 egg yolks

2 cups water

1 cup panko

1 cup all-purpose flour

Canola or vegetable oil

Special Supplies

Musubi mold (can be found online)

To make the musubi:

1. Cut the SPAM® into 8 to 10 slices and place them in a large bowl. Add the oyster sauce, soy sauce, and brown sugar over the SPAM®. Let this mixture sit for about 15 minutes.

2. In a medium frying pan over medium heat, fry the SPAM® on each side, until slightly crispy or until the SPAM® is at your desired crispiness level, about 1 to 2 minutes on each side. Set aside.

3. Crack the eggs in a medium bowl and whisk until well combined. In the same pan you cooked the SPAM® in, add the eggs. Without stirring, cook the scrambled eggs over low to medium heat, about 3 minutes. The goal is to make them flat, not fluffy. When the eggs are done, cut them into the size of a SPAM® slice.

4. Place one strip of nori on a clean work surface. Place your musubi mold across the middle of the nori. Add some rice to the mold, pressing down firmly and evenly, so there is about 1 to 1½ inches of rice on top of the nori. (Note: To prevent sticking, dip the mold and your fingers in water as you go.)

5. Remove the rice from the mold.

6. Add a pickle slice on top of your musubi, or enough pickle to cover the surface of the rice. Then add a slice of the cooked SPAM® and a piece of scrambled egg to the top.

7. Fold over side of the nori and stick it to the top of the SPAM®, then fold over the other side—just like you are wrapping a package for a friend. If needed, wet your finger with water to seal the nori.

8. Refrigerate the musubis for 1 hour.

continued on page 52

continued from page 51

To make the batter:

9. In a medium bowl, combine the egg yolks and water. In a second medium bowl, combine the panko and flour.

10. Take each musubi and dip each side in the egg wash bowl and then dip each side in the flour bowl.

11. Heat the oil on medium-high until it boils. Place the musubis in the oil, a few at a time, and cook for 2 to 3 minutes on each side. (Note: Use tongs to flip so the musubi doesn't fall apart.)

12. Set the musubis aside and let sit on a paper towel to drain excess oil.

13. Slice each musubi in 4 equal pieces and sprinkle paprika, if desired.

Braddah's Baked Spaghetti

Stitch is a voracious eater, and he isn't afraid of mixing up what he puts in his meal: batteries, trash, some fish bones . . . or in this case, a variety of meats and pineapple! The spaghetti version of a meat lover's pizza, this "plate lunch" is standard at any local restaurant in Hawai'i.

Prep Time: 20 minutes
Cook Time: 20 minutes
Servings: 5 to 6

1 tablespoon olive oil

1 small red onion, finely chopped

2 cloves garlic, minced

1 pound lean ground beef or turkey

One 32-ounce jar spaghetti sauce of choice

1 cup water

One 16-ounce package spaghetti

2 cups shredded Italian blend cheese

3 Portuguese sausages, sliced

4 Hawaiian Winners hot dogs, or 4 kosher hot dogs, sliced

1 small pineapple, skinned, cored, and sliced, or 1 to 2 cans sliced pineapple

1. Preheat the oven to 350°F.

2. In a large skillet or saucepan, heat the oil over medium heat. Add the onion and garlic and cook, stirring, for about 2 minutes.

3. Add the ground beef or turkey to the pan and cook until the meat is browned, 5 to 6 minutes. Drain the excess oil from the meat.

4. Add the spaghetti sauce and water to the pan, stirring constantly until heated through.

5. Grease a 2-quart casserole dish or lasagna pan. Pour a third of the sauce in the dish to cover the bottom.

6. Break the spaghetti in half, then lay one half evenly in the casserole dish.

7. Pour another third of the remaining sauce over the broken spaghetti noodles and sprinkle with 1 cup of the cheese.

8. Repeat layering the dish with the remaining half of the spaghetti and the remaining sauce; top with the sausages, hot dogs, and pineapple; finally add the remaining 1 cup of cheese on top.

9. Cover and bake for 20 minutes.

10. Uncover and bake for another 20 minutes, or until the cheese is lightly golden on top.

11. Remove your baked spaghetti from the oven and let sit for at least 5 minutes before serving.

Meteoric Teriyaki Chicken Skewers

Chickens can be hard to catch, but with his plasma pistol, Captain Gantu easily shoots nets to catch the pesky critters. A quick cook on the grill and he's got a tasty meal on his hands! This delicious dish is finished off with a bit of fire and flare.

Prep Time: 30 minutes, plus at least 30 minutes to marinate

Cook Time: 6 to 8 minutes

Servings: 4

1 tablespoon cornstarch

1¼ cups water, divided

½ teaspoon ground ginger

2 tablespoons honey

¼ cup soy sauce

¼ cup brown sugar

½ teaspoon garlic powder

2 pounds boneless skinless chicken breasts, cut into bite-sized pieces

1 tablespoon toasted sesame seeds

2 tablespoons chopped green onions

Special Supplies

Skewers, wood or metal

1. Whisk together the cornstarch and ¼ cup of water in a small bowl.

2. In a medium saucepan over medium heat, bring the ginger, honey, soy sauce, brown sugar, garlic powder, and remaining 1 cup of water to a simmer over medium heat.

3. Stir in the cornstarch mixture until it thickens enough to coat the back of a spoon, about 2 minutes. Cool to room temperature.

4. Place the chicken in a large bowl or resealable plastic bag and add the marinade you created.

5. Marinate the chicken for at least 30 minutes, or overnight, in the refrigerator.

6. Heat an outdoor grill to medium-high heat (375° to 450°F). (Note: If you do not have a grill, simply use a large pan or cast iron pan over medium-high heat.)

7. Thread the chicken onto the skewers.

8. Place the skewers on the grill and cook for 3 to 4 minutes on each side, until the chicken is cooked through.

9. Sprinkle the skewers with the sesame seeds and green onions and serve.

Royal Pūlehu Steak

When David puts on a fire show, he really puts on a show—flames everywhere!—which makes this flame-cooked dish a perfect option at the lūʻau! Fit for a king, this dish pays homage to the *paniolo*, or cattlemen, of Hawaiʻi. Even today, there are still a handful of ranches raising their cattle in the same traditions of old Hawaiʻi.

Prep Time: 20 minutes
Cook Time: 10 minutes
Servings: 4

Hawaiian Seasoning Salt

3 tablespoons Hawaiian salt

½ teaspoon garlic powder

½ teaspoon ground ginger

½ teaspoon freshly ground pepper

½ teaspoon onion powder

Steak

Two 8-ounce Paniolo Cattle Co. boneless rib eye steaks (Paniolo Cattle Co. is a product made on the Big Island of Hawaiʻi; find online or at major supermarkets, but you can use any rib eye of choice)

3 ounces avocado oil

8 slices thick-cut bacon

To make the Hawaiian seasoning salt:

1. In a small bowl, mix together the Hawaiian salt, garlic powder, ginger, pepper, and onion powder. Mix until well combined.

To make the steak:

2. Trim the excess fat along the edges of the steak. (Note: This will help prevent grill flare-ups and overcharring.) Pat the steak dry, then brush with the avocado oil.

3. Liberally season the steak with about 2 teaspoons of Hawaiian seasoning salt. Set aside and allow to rest 20 to 30 minutes prior to cooking.

4. Heat half of an outdoor grill to high, about 500°F. (Note: If you are using charcoal/wood, place it on half of the grill. If you are using electric burners, light half of the burners only.)

5. Place the steaks directly over the flame and sear one side for 3 to 5 minutes. Flip and repeat on the other side.

6. Move the steaks to the unlit side of the grill, close the lid, and cook until reaching your desired temperature. (See the cooking tips on page 11 for steak temperature tips.)

7. Remove the steaks from the grill and rest for 5 minutes before slicing.

8. Cook the bacon in a pan over high heat, to your desired crispiness.

9. Serve this delicious meal with a side of steamed white rice and a noodle salad, such as Nani's Spaghetti Salad (page 27), or serve it on top of your favorite greens, such as Mrs. Hasagawa's Garden Salad (page 76).

Sunset Grilled Pineapple Hamburger

Lilo loves experimenting in the kitchen. While some of her experiments end up looking—and tasting—more like science experiments gone wrong, this one is a real winner. A tasty burger covered in pineapple and bacon. How could this one *possibly* go wrong?

Prep Time: 20 minutes
Cook Time: 30 minutes
Servings: 4

Onions

2 tablespoons unsalted butter

1 Maui onion or sweet onion, thinly sliced

1 teaspoon Worcestershire sauce

Sea salt

Freshly ground pepper

1 tablespoon Dijon mustard

Burgers

4 strips thick-cut bacon

4 wide slices SPAM®, to cover the burger

1 pound Hawaiian grass-fed ground beef

Sea salt

Freshly ground pepper

1 fresh pineapple, sliced into rings

2 tablespoons barbecue sauce

4 slices white cheddar cheese

4 Hawaiian sweet bread buns, halved and toasted

1 tablespoon unsalted butter, or olive oil, for frying eggs

4 eggs

2 tablespoons Dijon mustard

4 leaves island butter lettuce (or any butter lettuce)

To make the onions:

1. Melt the butter in a small frying pan over medium heat.

2. Add the onions and sauté until softened, 3 to 5 minutes.

3. Add the Worcestershire and season with salt and pepper to taste. Stir to combine.

4. Reduce the heat to low and let the onions continue to cook, stirring occasionally. Cook until the onions look dark brown and caramelized, 15 to 30 minutes.

5. When onions are just about done, stir in the Dijon mustard for a tangy finish. Set aside while you prep the burgers.

continued on page 60

continued from page 59

To make the burgers:

6. Cook the bacon strips in the oven at 450°F until they are at your desired crispiness level and set aside.

7. Cook the SPAM® in a dry medium frying pan over medium heat until it reaches your desired level of crispiness.

8. Divide the ground beef into four portions and shape each portion into a patty. Season with salt and pepper to taste. Push a dent in the middle of each patty with your thumb to help them keep their shape while cooking.

9. Cook the burger patties in a large skillet over medium-high heat for 2 to 4 minutes per side, until they are cooked to your desired temperature (see cooking tips on page 11 for cooking temps). Alternatively, cook the burgers on an outdoor grill.

10. You can also grill the pineapple while the burgers are cooking. Simply add your pineapple slices to the grill and cook 2 to 3 minutes per side, or until golden brown. Set aside.

11. When burgers are almost ready, in the pan, top with a spoonful of the barbecue sauce and a slice of cheddar cheese. (Note: This will give the barbecue sauce and the cheese a chance to soak/melt into the meat.) Set the cooked burgers aside to rest while you prep the final ingredients.

12. Toast the Hawaiian bun halves.

13. Melt the butter in a large skillet over medium heat. (Note: You can use the same pan you cooked the burgers in for extra flavor.)

14. Crack the eggs into the skillet and fry until the whites are cooked through and yolks are slightly runny, 4 to 6 minutes.

15. To assemble, add the mustard to the bottom toasted bun, followed by lettuce, the burger patty (with the sauce and cheese), onions, bacon, SPAM®, egg, and pineapple. Enjoy the deliciousness that awaits you!

Pelekai Sweet and Sour Pork

Life has been tough for Lilo. As much as she loves Nani, she still misses her parents terribly. But this meal, passed down from generation to generation of the Pelekai family, always gives her a lift. Blending together Chinese and island flavors, this dish is a favorite among Hawaiian families, with each new generation adding their own unique touch of deliciousness.

Prep Time: 10 minutes, plus 40 minutes to marinate

Cook Time: 40 minutes

Servings: 4

Sweet and Sour Sauce

1 cup water

½ cup ketchup

½ cup rice vinegar

½ cup granulated sugar

½ tablespoon potato starch, mixed with 1 tablespoon water

Kosher salt

Pork Marinade

1 pound pork tenderloin, cut into 1-inch cubes

1½ tablespoons soy sauce (use low sodium soy sauce if desired)

1 tablespoon rice wine

½ teaspoon five-spice powder

¼ teaspoon freshly ground white pepper

2 cloves garlic, minced

1 large egg

3 tablespoons corn flour, or cornstarch

1 tablespoon all-purpose flour

Stir-Fry

3 cups plus 1 tablespoon neutral cooking oil

1 clove garlic, sliced

½ small white onion, finely diced

½ yellow bell pepper, cut into 1-inch diamond shapes

½ green bell pepper, cut into 1-inch diamond shapes

1 large mango, cut into chunks

2 large tomatoes, sliced at an angle like you would cut apples

½ fresh pineapple, cut into 1-inch chunks

½ tablespoon white sesame seeds

continued on page 64

continued from page 63

To make the sweet and sour sauce:

1. Combine the water, ketchup, rice vinegar, sugar, and potato starchy slurry in a medium saucepan and stir to mix evenly. Season with salt to taste. Place over medium-high heat.

2. Stirring constantly, bring the sauce to a boil and then reduce the heat to low and maintain a simmer.

3. Continue to stir the sauce until the texture has turned thick and sticky, about 25 minutes.

To make the pork marinade:

4. Place the pork in a bowl and add the soy sauce, rice wine, five-spice powder, white pepper, and garlic. Marinate for 10 minutes.

5. Add the egg, corn flour, and all-purpose flour to the pork marinade and mix evenly. Place in the refrigerator for 30 minutes.

To make the stir-fry:

6. Heat 3 cups of oil to 325°F in a large wok or deep saucepan over medium heat.

7. Gently slide in some of the pork tenderloin cubes, without overcrowding, and fry until golden brown in color, stirring occasionally, about 4 minutes per side. You can work with the pork in batches, if necessary.

8. Make sure the oil comes back up to temperature before each batch.

9. Place the cooked pork on a plate lined with a couple of sheets of paper towel.

10. Add the remaining 1 tablespoon of oil to the wok and stir-fry the garlic and onion over medium-high heat until fragrant.

11. Add the bell peppers, mangoes, tomatoes, and pineapple to the wok and stir-fry for 1 to 2 minutes.

12. Return the pork to the wok, along with the sweet and sour sauce, and mix evenly. You can add as much sweet and sour sauce as you prefer.

13. Garnish with the sesame seeds and serve.

Lawai'a Steamed Snapper

Lilo knows not to mess with Pudge the fish. But that doesn't mean the other fish in the ocean aren't fair game! Originally a Chinese preparation, this dish has become a staple in many households—especially those of Hawai'i's fishermen, or lawai'a.

Prep Time: 10 minutes
Cook Time: 25 minutes
Servings: 4

1 pound unpeeled Okinawan sweet potatoes (or purple yams)

4 ounces baby won bok (Napa cabbage)

Four 7-ounce red snapper fillets

1 pinch sea salt

1 pinch freshly ground pepper

3 ti leaves, or 1 banana leaf

2 ounces shiitake mushrooms, stemmed and thinly sliced

2 whole green onions, cut into diagonal slivers

1 tablespoon minced fresh ginger

20 leaves fresh cilantro, chopped

1 cup peanut oil

1 cup soy sauce, plus more for garnish

1. Place the sweet potatoes in a steaming grid, then place the grid in a large enough pot with water. Make sure the water doesn't touch the steaming grid (it cannot touch the potatoes). Cover and steam for 5 minutes, or until tender. Then, add the baby won bok and steam for 5 minutes, or until just tender. Set aside.

2. Season the red snapper with the salt and pepper and place (skin-side up) in the steamer over boiling water.

3. Cut the ti leaves the same size as the steamer (see the cooking tips on page 11 for how to wash and prep your ti leaves), and line the steamer with the leaves.

4. Cover and steam 10 to 15 minutes, or until the snapper is opaque throughout.

5. Remove the fish from the steamer and place on a metal rack, over a shallow pan to catch the drippings.

6. Top the snapper with the mushrooms, green onion, ginger, and cilantro.

7. Combine the peanut oil and soy sauce in a medium saucepan, and heat over high heat. When it's close to smoking, you know it's ready.

8. Pour the mixture over the fish very carefully, as it will be hot.

9. To plate the dish, arrange some of the steamed won bok in the center of each plate.

10. Place a snapper fillet with the veggies on top of each plate, then drizzle some of the pan drippings over the top of the fish.

11. Then place 2 pieces of the sweet potato at one end of each fish on the plate.

12. Sprinkle a little bit of soy sauce over each piece of fish and enjoy!

Lilo and Friends' Hawaiian Pizza

Lilo's friends, the children—or *keiki*—from dance class, bring a lot of unique flavors to the table, just like this pizza. When Lilo and her friends work up quite an appetite at dance class, this pizza is a great way to satisfy that hunger!

Prep Time: 30 minutes
Cook Time: 15 minutes
Servings: 8 slices

2 teaspoons minced garlic

2 teaspoons minced fresh ginger

2 teaspoons canola oil

1 pinch kosher salt

½ cup tomato purée

One 10- to 12-inch prepared pizza crust

½ cup all-purpose flour, for dusting

½ cup cornmeal, for dusting

1½ cups shredded cheese blend (mozzarella, provolone, cheddar, and/or Parmesan)

½ cup sliced pepperoni

½ cup chopped thick-cut bacon, uncooked

½ cup sliced mango

½ cup sliced honeydew melon

½ cup chopped fresh pineapple

1. Place an upside-down baking sheet in the oven and preheat both to 500°F.

2. In a food processor, pulse the garlic, ginger, canola oil, and salt until smooth to create a paste.

3. Mix 1 teaspoon of the garlic-ginger paste with the tomato purée. Set aside.

4. Flour the surface of the prepared pizza crust. Dust an upside-down baking sheet with cornmeal.

5. Put the crust on the cornmeal-dusted, upside-down baking sheet and slide onto the hot baking sheet already in the oven. Cook for 5 minutes.

6. Once it's cooked, spread the crust with the tomato purée. Then top with the cheese, pepperoni, bacon, mango, honeydew, and pineapple.

7. Return your pizza to the oven and bake until the cheese melts and the bacon cooks, about 8 to 10 more minutes.

8. Once the pizza is cooked, let it sit 5 minutes.

9. To serve, cut the pizza into 8 slices and enjoy with your favorite beverage.

CHAPTER
3

MULTI-GALACTIC PŪPŪS

626 Experimental Fried Rice

An experiment gone wrong—or is it right?—Stitch is a mix of parts from other species. But a hodgepodge isn't necessarily a bad thing, especially when it comes to fried rice! A traditional meal blended with sweet fresh fruits and crunchy pickled vegetables, this dish is a bit like Stitch: bold but enjoyable!

Prep Time: 15 to 20 minutes, plus 24 hours to refrigerate (or freeze)

Cook Time: 5 minutes

Servings: 4

4 cups cooked medium-grain rice

½ cup diced Portuguese sausage

2 slices bacon, diced

½ cup chopped green onions

½ cup diced Korean pears

½ cup bean sprouts

½ cup cucumber kimchee

½ cup frozen peas and carrots, thawed

½ cup chopped char siu pork

4 tablespoons oyster sauce

1 teaspoon sea salt

2 tablespoons hon dashi (Japanese bonito fish stock powder)

1. Dry the rice in the refrigerator or freezer for 24 hours by storing it covered. (Note: This is a local technique used by Hawaiian chefs; it keeps the grains from being overly soggy and prevents them from sticking.)

2. Brown the sausage and bacon in a large skillet over medium-high heat, about 5 minutes.

3. Add the dry rice to the skillet and mix well.

4. Add the green onions, pears, bean sprouts, kimchee, peas and carrots, and char siu, and mix together.

5. Add the oyster sauce, salt, and hon dashi and serve family style.

Li Hing Mui Grilled Pineapple and Mangoes

Lilo knows that after a day of biking around the island, there's nothing more refreshing than some fresh island fruit. Ripe mangoes and sweet pineapples from Mrs. Hasagawa's fruit stand mixed with dried and ground Chinese plums make for a delicious local treat.

Prep Time: 30 minutes

Cook Time: 4 to 6 minutes

Servings: 4 to 8

½ teaspoon li hing mui (Chinese red rock salt plums) powder

¼ teaspoon togarashi (Japanese seven-spice pepper powder)

1 pineapple, peeled and cut into spears

2 medium, half-ripe mangoes, peeled and cut into thick spears

2 tablespoons olive oil

½ tablespoon chopped fresh cilantro for garnishing, optional

1. Heat an outdoor grill to medium heat (350° to 375°F). (Note: If you don't have a grill, a large frying pan or an electric grill will be fine.)

2. Mix the li hing mui powder and togarashi together in a mixing cup.

3. Lightly brush all of the pineapple and mango with olive oil.

4. Place the fruit on the grill for 2 to 3 minutes total, flipping halfway through. Be sure to monitor that the fruit is not drying out.

5. Transfer the grilled fruit to a plate and dust with the powder mix.

6. Garnish with the cilantro, if desired.

Pleakley's Pickled Artifacts

A curious sort, Pleakley loves categorizing the many wonders of Earth. In fact, it wouldn't be surprising to find him keeping specimens in jars . . . much like those used to house this deliciously pickled treat. Or perhaps it's just that the alien look of pickled fruits makes Pleakley feel more at home. Either way, this staple of Hawaiian homes is one not to be missed.

Prep Time: 10 minutes

Cook Time: 10 minutes, plus 24 hours to pickle

Servings: 4 to 5

8 cups green mango, peeled and sliced

8 li hing mui (Chinese red rock salt plums)

1 tablespoon li hing mui powder

½ cup rice vinegar

½ cup apple cider vinegar

2 cups sugar

¼ cup Hawaiian salt

1 pint of your favorite ice cream, for serving

1. Put all the mango slices in a large bowl.

2. Add the li hing mui and li hing mui powder to the bowl.

3. Toss the mangoes in the powder so that everything is evenly coated.

4. In a medium saucepan over medium heat, combine the rice vinegar, apple cider vinegar, sugar, and salt. Bring everything to a boil, stirring until the sugar and salt are dissolved. Remove from the heat and cool for 5 minutes.

5. Pour the cool liquid over the bowl of mangoes. Let cool.

6. Transfer the mangoes to jars and store in the refrigerator for 24 hours before eating. (Note: Make sure to put the li hing seeds inside the jars when storing for extra flavor.)

7. To serve, add a couple scoops of your favorite ice cream and enjoy.

Mrs. Hasagawa's Garden Salad

Mrs. Hasagawa may be a bit forgetful, but she's got the best fruits and vegetables in town! There's nowhere else Nani would rather shop—although Stitch's antics may have made returning a little tough. This tasty mix of island treats can easily be found in Mrs. Hasagawa's market or anywhere in Hawai'i.

Prep and Cook Time:
30 to 40 minutes

Servings: 4

Miso Dressing

1 tablespoon white miso

2 tablespoons rice vinegar

1 tablespoon fresh lemon juice

½ teaspoon grated fresh ginger

1 small clove garlic, pressed

1 pinch cayenne pepper

2 tablespoons sesame oil

2 tablespoons peanut oil

2 tablespoons plain tzatziki yogurt

Salad

1½ heads crisp Mānoa lettuce, cleaned

12 to 16 sweet grape or cherry tomatoes, halved lengthwise

4 small spears fresh pineapple, diced

1 ripe avocado, split, pitted, quartered, then diced

2 small Japanese cucumbers, chopped

1 boiled/cooked Okinawan sweet potato (or purple yams), peeled and cut into chunks

4 ounces Hawaiian goat cheese, crumbled

To make the miso dressing:

1. Combine the miso, rice vinegar, and lemon juice in a small bowl and whisk together. Add the ginger, garlic, cayenne pepper, sesame oil, peanut oil, and yogurt. Whisk until combined.

To assemble the salad:

2. Divide the lettuce between four salad bowls and add the tomatoes, pineapple, avocado, cucumbers, sweet potato, and goat cheese on top.

3. Drizzle with the miso dressing and enjoy.

Black and Blue Grilled 'Ahi with Experimental Sweet Potato Mush

If there's one thing Lilo loves to eat at the lū'au, it's sweet potatoes—even if she does sometimes get a bit distracted with showing Stitch his mischief level. These vibrant purple Okinawan sweet potatoes pair excellently with the star of the dish, 'ahi tuna, an all-time favorite in Hawai'i.

Prep Time: 10 minutes

Cook Time: 20 minutes

Servings: 6

Six 6-ounce 'ahi tuna steaks

3 pounds Okinawan sweet potatoes (or purple yams), peeled

4 tablespoons unsalted butter

½ cup whole milk

8 ounces sour cream

1 tablespoon minced garlic

¼ teaspoon freshly ground pepper

1 to 2 teaspoons garlic powder

1 to 2 teaspoons sea salt

1. Generously apply salt and pepper to both sides of the 'ahi steaks.

2. Heat an outdoor grill to medium heat (350° to 375°F). Add the tuna steaks and cook for 1 to 2 minutes on each side, until they are seared but not cooked all the way through. (Some call this "black and blue style," whereas Hawaiians call it "just right!") If you don't have a grill, simply use a small frying pan over medium heat, and cook the tuna one by one the same way, lightly cooked on each side. Of course, please cook the 'ahi tuna steaks to your desired temperature.

3. Quarter the sweet potatoes.

4. Place the potatoes in a large pot and cover with water (water should come 1 inch above potatoes).

continued on page 80

79

continued from page 79

5. Bring the potatoes to a boil over high heat. Once boiling, reduce the heat to medium-high.

6. Boil for 10 to 12 minutes, or until the potatoes are easily pierced in the center by a fork.

7. Drain the water and transfer potatoes to a large bowl.

8. Add the butter, milk, sour cream, garlic, and pepper. Add the garlic powder and salt to taste.

9. Use a potato masher or a hand mixer to mash the potatoes until all ingredients are combined and the potatoes are smooth.

10. To serve, plate the dish with a big scoop of the purple mash in the center and top with one piece of 'ahi steak. Enjoy!

Traditional Lomilomi Salmon

Lomilomi means "to knead or rub" in Hawaiian—in this case, rubbing salt into salmon. But all that rubbing requires a lot of hands. It's a good thing Stitch has so many! With two extra hands, this tasty dish will be ready in no time!

Prep and Cook Time:
1 hour and 20 minutes
Servings: 4 to 5

½ pound salmon

½ cup Hawaiian salt (apply as needed depending on your preferred saltiness level)

2 medium tomatoes

1 large Maui onion or sweet onion

6 green onions

1. Clean the salmon fillet and pat dry.

2. Sprinkle both sides of the salmon with the salt.

3. Put the salted salmon in a glass tray and wrap with plastic. Refrigerate the salmon for 3 days.

4. Before preparing the lomilomi, wash the salted salmon and soak it in a bowl of cold water for 1 hour. Pat dry before cutting.

5. Dice the salted salmon, tomatoes, onion, and green onions separately. The goal is to create bite-sized pieces (much smaller than poke, but more like a thick salsa or ceviche).

6. Place all of the chopped ingredients together into a big bowl and stir gently.

7. With your hands, gently mix the ingredients together until well combined. Add salt to taste.

8. Let chill in the refrigerator for 30 minutes, or dig right in like I usually do.

Pro Tip: You can also buy already salted/cured salmon at the grocery store to save you a few days.

CHAPTER
4

DECADENT DESSERTS

Pā'ina Haupia Cake

It turns out, Stitch is quite the baker. Just ask Lilo, who loved every bite of the birthday cake he made for her. Haupia is a coconut cream-based dessert that can be found at most parties. In fact, the word *pā'ina* means "party" in Hawaiian!

Prep Time: 30 minutes
Cook Time: 1½ hours
Servings: 4 to 5

Cake

Two 16¼-ounce boxes white cake mix

1 cup coconut milk, divided into thirds

⅔ cup water

6 egg whites

Frosting

1 teaspoon unflavored gelatin

1½ tablespoons cold coconut milk

12 ounces plus 1 teaspoon heavy whipping cream

¼ cup powdered sugar

1 teaspoon lemon extract

Filling

1 cup sugar

½ teaspoon sea salt

6 tablespoons cornstarch

1 cup water

4 cups full-fat coconut milk

2 teaspoons vanilla extract

Decorations

2 cups confectioners' sugar

1 egg white (or dried egg white)

½ teaspoon water, plus more as needed

Blue, black, and pink food coloring

½ cup shredded coconut

Special Supplies

6 piping bags

To make the cake:

1. Preheat the oven according to the directions on the cake mix box. Grease and flour two 8- or 9-inch round cake pans.

2. Bake the cake according to the package directions, usually 30 to 40 minutes, but instead of using the dairy milk or water, use the coconut milk.

3. As soon as the cakes are finished baking, cool and cut each one horizontally into two layers. If your top layers are shaped like a dome, cut them so they are flat. (Note: This is to keep your frosting and filling from spilling out.)

To make the frosting:

4. Soften the gelatin in a small bowl with the cold coconut milk, about 5 minutes. Once done, heat in the microwave for 5 seconds, or until fully melted. Let the gelatin cool completely and add 1 teaspoon of the heavy cream to help it combine in the next step.

5. In a medium bowl, whip the remaining 12 ounces of heavy cream. Fold in the powdered sugar and lemon extract. Once soft peaks appear, mix in the gelatin and mix at a higher speed until you have firm peaks. You've just made your frosting! Chill it in the fridge until it is easy to spread.

continued on page 86

continued from page 85

To make the filling:

6. In a small bowl, combine the sugar, salt, cornstarch, and water. Set aside.

7. In a medium saucepan over medium heat, heat up the coconut milk. When it's hot, add the sugar mixture you just made.

8. Cook the coconut-sugar mixture until it thickens, stirring constantly. Remove from the heat and stir in the vanilla. Let cool and chill the filling in the fridge until it's easy to spread.

To prepare the decorations:

9. In a small bowl, mix together the confectioners' sugar, egg white, and water until thickened and smooth, about 2 minutes, to create your royal icing. Add more water as needed. Once at the desired consistency, divide into 4 bowls, with one bowl containing half the total frosting.

10. Create a light blue icing using food coloring in the bowl with the most frosting and set aside a fourth of that in a piping bag. Next, add more blue food coloring to the same bowl to create the medium blue color icing and set aside three-fourths of that icing in a piping bag. With the remaining icing, add even more blue food coloring to get the darkest shade of blue and set aside in a piping bag.

11. The remaining 3 bowls of icing will need food coloring added to each to become the pink, black, and white icing colors. Once all are created, set aside each in piping bags. (Note: Black frosting can be more easily achieved with coco powder; add some additional water to smooth out the frosting again.)

12. Once all royal icing colors are made, you're ready to create your icing Stitch! Lay a piece of parchment flat on your counter with the Stitch illustration (see page 89) and begin by tracing with your black icing and then filling in each section with the appropriate color. When finished, set aside until fully dried and firm to the touch, which will take a few hours.

13. While your icing is drying, separate your shredded coconut into 3 portions. One portion should remain as it is and be left white, while the other 2 portions should be dyed with food coloring to create the darkest blue and then a medium blue for your coconut ombré.

To assemble the cake:

14. Spread the cake filling between each cake layer, spreading it on pretty thick—about ¼ to ½ inch or so.

15. Assemble the layers in this order: cake, filling, cake, filling, cake, filling, cake—until you are out of ingredients.

16. Refrigerate your assembled cake until it is set.

17. Once the cake is ready, frost the whole thing with your whipped cream mixture.

18. Sprinkle the shredded coconut all over the sides of the cake, starting with the darkest blue at the base, the medium shade of blue in the center, and white at the top.

19. Once your icing Stitch is dried, using a small spatula, carefully pull away the parchment paper and place Stitch on the top of your cake.

20. Keep refrigerated until ready to serve.

To create your own adorable Stitch detail, use a piece of transparent paper or wax paper to trace the illustration below for your cake.

Rock-a-Hula Açaí Bowls

Hawai'i and Elvis have a special connection, and Lilo and Stitch love listening to the king of rock and roll! They'd listen to Elvis all day if they could—especially Stitch, who looks great in a sequin jumpsuit. But singing and dancing is hungry work. What better way to refresh yourself than with a delicious, healthy açaí bowl? This tasty trend swept the islands, and it's here to stay!

Prep and Cook Time:
10 minutes
Servings: 1

Two 14-ounce packets unsweetened frozen açaí

1 frozen banana, cut into chunks

¼ cup nondairy milk (almond or oat)

½ cup frozen mixed berries

1 tablespoon peanut butter or nut butter of choice

1 scoop Greek yogurt

Any toppings of choice (e.g., a drizzle of crumbled macadamia nuts, granola, berries, banana slices, chia seeds, etc.)

1. Place the frozen açaí, banana chunks, milk, berries, peanut butter, and yogurt in a blender.

2. Put the lid on your blender and blend on low, slowly increasing speed as everything starts to combine.

3. Occasionally stop the blender and move around the contents, as some areas may still be more frozen than others.

4. Once everything is combined and smooth, scoop your blended smoothie into a bowl.

5. Add any other toppings of your choosing, such as macadamia nuts, granola, banana slices, or fresh fruit.

Luki's Shaved Ice

When Lilo meets Stitch, she can't wait to show him around town. And where better to start than at the shaved ice stand? Shaved ice is a delicious version of snow cones—but Hawaiian style—and some prefer the superfine "snow," while others love to have a crunch. Too bad for Stitch, his ends up on the head of a too-curious dog!

Prep Time: 1 hour

Cook Time: 15 minutes

Servings: 3 to 4

1½ cups various fruits of choice (e.g., strawberries, pineapple, mango, etc.)

2 tablespoons fresh lemon or lime juice

¾ cup water

¾ cup sugar

Ice, as needed

1 to 2 scoops vanilla ice cream

½ cup sweetened condensed milk

1. Clean all of your fruit and combine the fruit in a blender or food processor.

2. Pour the blended fruit into a medium saucepan and add the lemon juice, water, and sugar.

3. Cook the fruit mixture on medium heat, stirring occasionally until it begins to boil.

4. Turn the heat down low and let it simmer for 5 minutes before removing the pan from the heat.

5. Let the syrup cool completely, then pour the contents through a fine strainer or colander. Use the syrup immediately or store in a jar in the refrigerator.

6. To assemble, add ice cubes to a food processor and blend, 1 cup at a time, until the cubes look like snow with no lumps. Alternatively, you can use a shaved-ice machine to speed up the process.

7. Add a scoop of vanilla ice cream to each dish, then top with the shaved ice.

8. To serve, drizzle with the syrup you made and the sweetened condensed milk.

Fun Fact: A local favorite in Hawai'i is always the "Rainbow," which is a mixture of all flavors.

Guava Celebration Cake

Lilo loves ice cream. She'd eat it every day. But when it's a special occasion, it's time for a special treat. Enter the Guava Celebration Cake! This carefully layered cake contains deliciously sweet guava. Lilo had better watch out that Stitch doesn't find it first!

Prep Time: 10 minutes, plus cooling time

Cook Time: 40 minutes

Servings: 18 to 20

Cake

Two 15.25-ounce boxes strawberry cake mix

2⅔ cups guava nectar or guava juice

6 eggs

⅔ cup coconut oil, at room temperature (liquid)

Guava Gel Topping

2 cups guava nectar or guava juice

½ cup sugar

¼ cup cornstarch

3 tablespoons water

Cream Cheese Layer

16 ounces cream cheese, softened

⅔ cup sugar

2 teaspoons vanilla extract

16 ounces whipped cream (thawed if frozen)

Assembly

About 2 cups dried mangoes, cut in tall triangles

About 15 fresh strawberries, thinly sliced

continued on page 96

continued from page 95

To make the cake:

1. Preheat the oven to 350°F. Grease and flour a 9-inch square cake pan.

2. In a large bowl, combine the strawberry cake mix, guava nectar, eggs, and coconut oil. Mix until well combined. Pour the batter into the prepared cake pan.

3. Bake your cakes for about 30 to 40 minutes, or until a cake tester comes out clean.

4. Allow to cool completely before assembly.

To make the guava gel topping:

5. In a medium saucepan over medium heat, bring the guava nectar and sugar to a boil.

6. In a small bowl or measuring cup, mix the cornstarch and water.

7. Remove the guava nectar from the heat and stir in the cornstarch mixture.

8. Return the guava nectar back to heat and bring to a boil for 1 minute. Let the gel topping cool in the refrigerator.

To make the cream cheese layer:

9. In a medium bowl, whip the cream cheese until fluffy. (Note: A hand mixer may help with this.)

10. Add the sugar and vanilla, mixing well with a hand mixer. Fold the whipped cream in slowly. Then refrigerate until you are ready to assemble your cake.

To assemble the cake:

11. When the cake is cool, cut the cake in half horizontally to make two cake layers.

12. Lay the bottom layer and a cake board (or serving platter) on a surface, and use 1½ cups of the cream cheese frosting to frost the top, creating a filling, spreading smoothly to the edges. Cover the frosting with 1 cup of the guava gel, again spreading smoothly to the edges.

13. Place the second layer of cake on top and use the remaining cream cheese mixture to frost the top and sides of the cake, coating it completely. Refrigerate until ready to serve.

14. Up to 1 hour before serving, decorate the cake with the mangoes and strawberries, alternating along the top edge of the cake to create a crown. Refrigerate until serving.

Mahalo Hasagawa Matcha Brownies

Family celebrations like Thanksgiving and Christmas wouldn't be complete without dessert, and for Lilo and Stitch, that's these delicious brownies that Mrs. Hasagawa would love. Mrs. Hasagawa has a sweet tooth and loves to incorporate her Japanese heritage with her sweet treats. This special dessert—featuring Japanese matcha, a traditional green tea that is often found in powder form—is the perfect treat to thank the ever-generous Mrs. Hasagawa for her delicious fruit and vegetable stands.

Prep Time: 10 minutes, plus 30 minutes to cool

Cook Time: 30 to 40 minutes

Servings: 3 to 4

2 cups white chocolate chips, divided

4 ounces unsalted butter

3 eggs

1 teaspoon vanilla extract

1 cup white sugar

¼ cup brown sugar

1 cup all-purpose flour

2 tablespoons matcha powder

½ teaspoon sea salt

Powdered sugar for dusting, optional

1. Preheat the oven to 350°F. Line an 8-inch square pan with parchment paper.

2. Melt 1 cup of the white chocolate chips and the butter, slowly, in a medium saucepan over low heat. (Note: You can also melt the chips and butter in the microwave, too.)

3. In a small bowl, beat the eggs, adding in the vanilla extract, the sugars, and the melted chocolate.

4. Sift in the flour, followed by the matcha and salt, and mix into the batter until smooth. Stir in the remaining 1 cup of white chocolate chips.

5. Transfer the batter to the prepared pan. Bake for 20 to 30 minutes. Poke the center with a toothpick. When the toothpick comes out completely clean, it's ready.

6. Let the brownies cool for 30 minutes, then slice into an even number of pieces. Dust with powdered sugar, if desired. Enjoy with those for whom you are thankful.

Comforting Butter Mochi

Taking care of Lilo is hard work, and sometimes Nani isn't sure she is doing everything right. But a slice of her Butter Mochi always cheers her up. After all, who could stay down with a warm piece of comforting mochi?

Prep Time: 15 minutes
Cook Time: 1 hour
Servings: 4 to 5

One 16-ounce box mochiko flour (can be found online)

2 cups granulated sugar

1 teaspoon baking powder

4 large eggs, at room temperature

2 cups whole milk

One 12-ounce can coconut milk

¾ cup unsalted butter, softened

2 teaspoons vanilla extract

1. Preheat the oven to 350°F.

2. Grease a 9-by-13-inch baking pan and line with parchment paper.

3. In a large bowl, mix together the mochiko flour, sugar, and baking powder.

4. Add the eggs, followed by the whole milk, coconut milk, butter, and vanilla. Using an electric mixer, or by hand, whisk together to form a smooth batter. Pour this mixture into the pan you prepared.

5. Bake for 50 to 60 minutes, or until golden brown on top. Set the mochi aside to cool down completely.

6. Cut into equal squares and serve.

Po'ipū Poi Mochi

Very similar to a traditional donut or a Portuguese malasada, this version of mochi is made with poi from kalo, also known as taro. Poi is created by pounding the root of the taro plant with a volcanic mortar and water. In Hawaiian, *po'ipū* means "crashing waves," and as the Hawaiian locals like to say, "The waves were pounding near Po'ipū." Instead of pounding your own poi, you can also find ready-made poi in all Hawaiian grocery stores and, of course, online in frozen form.

Prep Time: 10 minutes
Cook Time: 10 minutes
Servings: 4 to 5

1 pound poi (found in the frozen section of your grocery store or online)

Two 10-ounce packages mochiko

1 tablespoon ground cinnamon

1 teaspoon sea salt

1½ cups sugar

2 cups water

1 quart canola oil, for deep-frying

1 sprinkle powdered sugar or ground cinnamon, optional

1. In a small bowl, mix the poi, mochiko, cinnamon, salt, and sugar together. Add the water slowly, until mixture is similar to the consistency of muffin batter.

2. In a large pan or Dutch oven, heat the oil to 365° to 375°F.

3. Drop teaspoonfuls of the mixture into the oil and fry until the outside is slightly crisp, about 4 minutes.

4. Drain the mochi on absorbent paper towels before serving. Traditionally, poi mochi is served after the oil is drained, but you can also add a sprinkle of powdered sugar or cinnamon on top, if desired.

Ube Ice Cream

After a hot day on the beach, there's nothing more refreshing than some ice cream. (Just ask the poor tourist who lost his in the chaos of Stitch playing Elvis!) For a true Hawaiian treat, try out ube ice cream, which gets its flavor from a purple Southeast Asian yam. With its out-of-this-world color, this cooling treat is sure to be celebrated from one galaxy to another.

Prep and Cook Time: 10 minutes, plus at least 5 hours to freeze

Servings: 4 to 5

2 cups heavy whipping cream, cold

One 14-ounce can sweetened condensed milk, cold

4 teaspoons ube flavoring extract

1 tablespoon ube powder

Luki's Shaved Ice (page 92), optional

Flavored syrups, optional

Toasted coconut flakes for topping, optional

1. Using a handheld mixer, whip the heavy cream on medium-high speed until soft peaks form.

2. Pour in the condensed milk and whip until thick, stiff peaks form.

3. Add the ube extract and powder, then whip until combined.

4. Spread the whipped mixture evenly into a freezer-safe container, cover, and freeze for at least 5 hours, or overnight.

5. Take 1 or 2 scoops of ube, add 1 or 2 scoops of shaved ice (optional but delicious), and top the ice cream with your favorite syrup, if using.

6. If desired, sprinkle toasted coconut flakes on top to serve.

CHAPTER
5

SIPS IN PARADISE

Blue Hawaiian

A favorite of Lilo's, who is particularly fond of Elvis's "Blue Suede Shoes," this drink originated at the Hilton Hawaiian Village and was created by Harry Yee for the Bols company. It is still the most famous and favorite drink to have at a lūʻau, but this one can be enjoyed by the whole family!

Prep and Cook Time:
5 minutes

Servings: 2 to 4

½ cup fresh lemon juice

½ cup simple syrup

1½ cups pineapple juice

1 cup coconut water

2 teaspoons blue vanilla syrup

2 to 4 pineapple slices, with the rind left on

2 to 4 maraschino cherries

Special Supplies

Tropical glassware, optional

Silly long straw, optional

1. Combine the lemon juice, simple syrup, pineapple juice, coconut water, and blue vanilla syrup together in a glass, then shake until mixed.

2. Strain into a tropical glass, if using, over ice.

3. To garnish, place a pineapple slice on the glass, then add a silly long straw if using, and a maraschino cherry.

The Green Flash

Lilo and Stitch love watching the sunset from the comfort of their hammock. The mysterious green light that flashes as the sun sets reminds them of when Stitch first landed in Hawai'i. This green drink is for sure out of this world!

Prep and Cook Time:
5 minutes

Servings: 2 to 4

¼ cup fresh lemon juice

1 cup pineapple juice

½ cup ginger syrup

2 to 3 ounces green apple soda

Special Supplies

Transparent tiki glass (or something you can easily see through), optional

Parasol, optional

Silly straw, optional

1. Pour the lemon juice, pineapple juice, ginger syrup, and green apple soda into the glass with ice and stir slightly.

2. To garnish, place a parasol and silly straw if desired.

Pro Tip: Place a glow cube switched to a non-pulsing white light color for an out-of-this-world light show in your drink.

Coconut Coastal Delight

David, along with most surfers in Hawai'i, loves catching some waves as the sun sets over the island. A refreshing Coconut Coastal Delight on the sand is the perfect way to say goodbye to the waves until the next morning.

Prep and Cook Time:
5 minutes

Servings: 2 to 4

¼ cup coconut syrup

3 tablespoons fresh lime juice

¼ cup pineapple juice

¾ cup coconut water

4 to 6 ounces ginger beer

2 to 4 mint sprigs

Special Supplies

Precut and cored coconut or a coconut tiki mug, optional

Silly straw of any kind, optional

1. Combine the coconut syrup, lime juice, pineapple juice, coconut water, and some ice in a glass, mix together, and strain into a coconut vessel, if using, filled with new ice (instead of pouring all the contents in).

2. Fill the rest of the vessel with ginger beer and slightly stir.

3. Garnish with a silly straw, if using, and mint sprig.

Pink and Blue Sunset

When Nani isn't working, she loves to walk along the beach and watch the sunset with Lilo as she sings her "Aloha 'Oe," a beautiful song that means "Farewell to Thee" written by Princess Lili'uokalani in 1878. But for those times when she can't make it out to the beach, this pink and blue drink tides her over until the next day. And speaking of tides, a high tide at sunset is a surfer's dream.

Prep and Cook Time:
5 minutes
Servings: 2

¼ cup yuzu juice

¾ cup lehua honey syrup (mix 2 parts honey with 1 part water)

¾ cup cranberry juice

¾ cup nonalcoholic white cane spirit

2 tablespoons blueberry syrup

8 fresh blueberries, 4 per drink

Special Supplies

Bamboo pick

1. In a cocktail shaker, shake the yuzu juice, lehua honey syrup, cranberry juice, and nonalcoholic white cane spirit with ice, then strain into a chilled glass of choice.

2. Take 1 tablespoon of the blueberry syrup and pour directly into the center of the drink so that it settles at the bottom of the glass.

3. To garnish, add a bamboo pick with 4 large blueberries to your glass.

Island Grilled Lemonade

The first time Cobra Bubbles comes to visit, Nani offers him a nice, cool glass of lemonade. Too bad for Mr. Bubbles, this grilled lemonade is so delicious that it's already gone by the time he gets there!

Prep Time: 10 minutes
Cook Time: 5 minutes
Servings: 2 to 4

10 fresh lemons

1 cup sugar

8 ounces lehua honey (Hawaiian honey made from lehua blossoms)

1 gallon water

Special Supplies

Lightbulb glass (or any round or bulb-shaped glass), optional

1. Halve the lemons and sprinkle sugar over the cut sides.

2. Place the sugared lemons on a grill or in a large skillet over medium heat.

3. Grill the lemons until there are visible grill lines, if you are using a grill. If you are using a skillet, cook until you hear the lemon sizzling and they turn slightly brown, about 3 minutes.

4. Remove the lemons from the heat and let sit for 5 minutes.

5. In a large pitcher, squeeze the lemons and strain the juice to remove the pulp.

6. Add the honey and the full gallon of water to a pot and simmer on the stove. Stir the water until the honey dissolves completely.

7. Pour the honey water into the pitcher with the grilled lemon juice, and combine by continuously stirring.

8. Add about 6 ounces of water to the existing contents. Stir thoroughly.

9. Let the lemonade chill in the fridge, or add ice to enjoy immediately.

10. Place empty lemon skins into your lemonade container to let the cooked lemon peels bond and blend with the lemonade. Serve in a light bulb glass, if using. Sip and enjoy!

Pleakley's Pink Stuff Frosé

Pleakley is an explorer, but he still misses the sunsets back home. This delicious pink drink reminds him of watching them with his mother.

Prep and Cook Time:
7 minutes
Servings: 4

8 ounces pink lemonade

3 large strawberries, with the tops cut off

½ cup bite-sized pieces fresh watermelon

½ ounce simple syrup

2 cups ice

2 cups sparkling apple cider

4 thinly sliced lemon wheels

Special Supplies

Mason jars, optional

1. Combine the pink lemonade, strawberries, watermelon, and simple syrup in a blender with ice, then blend until you get a slushy consistency.

2. Add more ice if the consistency is too watery.

3. Pour your blended mixture into the mason jars, if using.

4. Top with the sparkling apple cider.

5. To garnish, place a lemon wheel on the rim of the glass.

Dietary Considerations

Measurement Conversion Charts

Volume

CUP	OZ	TBSP	TSP	ML
1	8	16	48	240
3/4	6	12	36	180
2/3	5	11	32	160
1/2	4	8	24	120
1/3	3	5	16	80
1/4	2	4	12	60

Temperatures

°F	°C
200°	93.3°
250°	120°
275°	135°
300°	150°
325°	165°
350°	177°

Weight

US	METRIC
0.5 OZ	14 G
1 OZ	28 G
¼ LB	113 G
⅓ LB	151 G
½ LB	227 G
1 LB	454 G

Acknowledgments

Aloha, friends! I hope you enjoyed your adventure through our delicious cookbook. When I was asked to write this book, I knew it would be a lot of fun, but what I didn't realize was how much the whole experience would take me back to the adorable and familiar scenes from the *Lilo and Stitch* movie.

Big MAHALO to Sammy Holland, who guided me through this uncharted journey of writing this book. And mahalo for my 'ohana: To my Mama Rena, who passed away a few years ago—she always kept us well fed and took care of my brothers and me while my parents worked hard providing for our family. Mahalo to my dad, Tim Sr., who I got most of my Japanese dishes from (he ran a very reputable Japanese restaurant), and my mom, who carried the torch of the family and passed down the recipes from each generation. To my uncle Ed, who (still, to this day) always cooks up a meal for us whenever we are home—that is an example of true island hospitality.

But my biggest inspiration, was my own keiki. *Keiki* is the Hawaiian word for "children." Not too often can generations enjoy the same food and movies growing up. *Lilo and Stitch* showed me that no matter how challenging life can be, your 'ohana will always be there for you and you for them. And since I was brought up as a Disney kid, I have passed along my love for the film and these recipes to my kids: Aloha and mahalo to Emerson, Mathias, Quinten, Madison, Makaleia, and Venessa. Now please enjoy your own family lūʻau, hopefully with a few of our inspiring dishes!

INSIGHT
EDITIONS

PO Box 3088
San Rafael, CA 94912
www.insighteditions.com

 Find us on Facebook: www.facebook.com/InsightEditions
𝕏 Follow us on X: @insighteditions

ISBN: 978-1-64722-957-3

Publisher: Raoul Goff
VP, Co-Publisher: Vanessa Lopez
VP, Creative: Chrissy Kwasnik
VP, Manufacturing: Alix Nicholaeff
VP, Group Managing Editor: Vicki Jaeger
Publishing Director: Jamie Thompson
Designer: Leah Bloise Lauer
Senior Editor: Sammy Holland
Editorial Assistant: Emma Merwin
Managing Editor: Maria Spano
Senior Production Editor: Katie Rokakis
Production Associate: Deena Hashem
Senior Production Manager, Subsidiary Rights: Lina s Palma-Temena

Lilo and Stitch **Headnote Consultant:** Brooke Vitale
Photographer: Ted Thomas
Food and Prop Stylist: Elena P. Craig
Assistant Food Stylist: August Craig
Assistant Baker: Megan Sinead Bingham
Photoshoot Art Direction: Judy Wiatrek Trum

 ®REPLANTED PAPER

Insight Editions, in association with Roots of Peace, will plant two trees for each tree used in the manufacturing of this book. Roots of Peace is an internationally renowned humanitarian organization dedicated to eradicating land mines worldwide and converting war-torn lands into productive farms and wildlife habitats. Roots of Peace will plant two million fruit and nut trees in Afghanistan and provide farmers there with the skills and support necessary for sustainable land use.

Manufactured in China by Insight Editions

10 9 8 7 6 5 4 3 2